RONALDO

RISE OF THE LEGEND

ROY BRANDON

Ronaldo: Rise Of The Legend
Copyright © 2016 by Roy Brandon.

CONTENTS

CHAPTER ONE

THE ICON

"I'm living a dream I never want to wake up from." –
Cristiano Ronaldo

CRISTIANO RONALDO IS A MODERN-DAY icon. On an almost daily basis we see hear his name on the news, see his face on any number of TV commercials, and marvel at the magic show he puts on every weekend when he takes to the field. He is a celebrity whose image and influence affect our popular culture and a soccer star that has been compared with some of the world's best athletes.

But Cristiano was not always the popular, mega-celebrity, soccer superstar that he is today. The success that he enjoys has come from years of hard work and sacrifice that have helped him overcome many obstacles and difficulties in his path. His hard work and determination are well known by other soccer celebrities. Jose Mourinho, his old coach at Real Madrid once said that "he is the best. The best in the world. Probably the best ever. I saw Maradona a couple of times, but Cristiano is amazing. The man is the best...Cristiano is a goal machine. He is an incredible player. Of this I am certain...there will never be another Cristiano Ronaldo."

His success on the soccer field has led him to become one of the highest paid athletes in all the world, some believe his contract to be the most expensive of all soccer players in the world. His fame has also landed him numerous advertisement deals with Nike and other famous brands of clothes, perfumes, cars and countless other products. Florentino Pérez, the president of the Real Madrid football club where Ronaldo plays, has made it clear that while he commands a high salary, it is clearly worth it, because as he states, "Cristiano is priceless."

If you have ever dreamed of being a soccer star like Cristiano Ronaldo, the first thing you'll need to do is be prepared to work hard. Ronaldo works out every day early in the morning. His training in the weight room emphasizes explosion, endurance, speed, strength and the functional movement needed on the field. He also spends hours every day at his soccer practices and workouts focusing on his footwork and ball control.

In 2015, Cristiano revealed a set of secrets

that he recommends to others to help them become the best they can be. He would tell you that in order to reach your full potential, you need to learn to train your mind as well as your body. Mental strength is just as important as physical strength and will help you achieve your goals. Furthermore, discipline is necessary to keep yourself motivated.

Cristiano also believes that it is important to set goals to help to keep you focused and working towards something specific. Working with a training partner is also good way to add a bit of competitiveness and help you to push yourself. If you train with someone who is at a similar level to yourself, then you will help push each other. Just make sure that training partner isn't Cristiano!

Cristiano also focuses on getting enough rest in order to get the most out of his training. He goes to bed early and gets up early, as sleep helps muscles recover. Ronaldo believes that training isn't only done on the field or in the weight room. His advice is to fit exercise into your life wherever you can. You can do an abs workout, for example, in your bedroom when you wake up in the morning or at night before you go to bed.

But working out isn't sufficient in itself, and must be combined with a good diet. Cristiano eats a high protein diet, with lots of wholegrain carbohydrates, fruit and vegetables and avoids sugary foods. If you train regularly, it is important to keep energy levels high in order to fuel your body for better performance. He sometimes eats up to six smaller meals a day to make sure he has enough energy to perform each session at a top level.

In this book, we're going to take a look at the life of Cristiano, beginning at the time he was rising star whose career was threatened by a strange heart condition, right up until his third Ballon D'or recognition. We will also follow Cristiano off of the field to see his impact on popular culture and his life beyond soccer.

CHAPTER TWO

THE POOR KID FROM THE NEIGHBORHOOD

"Today there are opportunities that no one knows if they will come round again in the future." – Cristiano Ronaldo

CRISTIANO RONALDO WAS BORN IN Portugal, in a small town called Funchal, in the province of Madeira. Madeira is a semi-autonomous island off of the coast of Portugal and Funchal is the largest city on the small island. Many people don´t know that

Ronaldo isn't really Cristiano's last name, but rather his second name. His full name is Cristiano Ronaldo dos Santos Aveiro. Ronaldo is his middle name and was given to him by his father who named him after his favorite American actor, Ronald Reagan, who later became president of the United States.

Cristiano's family came from humble beginnings. His great grandmother was from Cape Verde, off of the coast of Africa. His mother, Maria Dolores dos Santos Aveiro was a cook and his father, José Dinis Aveiro, was a gardener that worked for the local city government. Outside of watching games on the TV, neither of his parents had connections to the soccer world.

Cristiano has one old brother named Hugo and two older sisters, Elma and Liliano Catia. Despite having hard-working parents, his family struggled with poverty, and Cristiano had to share a room with his brother and sisters. To support the family, his father had to take on extra work as an equipment manager for a local, amateur soccer team called Andorinha. At eight years old, Cristiano began to play for this soccer club where his father was an employee. He quickly began to show signs of progress and ability. Only two years later he signed to play with Nacional, the local soccer team that plays in the Portuguese professional soccer league.

Even when he was young, soccer was a passion for Cristiano. His mother recalls that, "when he got home from school I'd tell him to do homework but he'd say he didn't have any. I'd be busy making dinner and he would jump out the window and run off until late," playing soccer. Strangely enough, Cristiano's nickname as a youngster was "cry baby." Again, his mother recalls that, "he used to cry when he passed and his friends didn't score. People called him 'cry-baby' and 'little bee,' because nobody could catch him."

Cristiano´s family was staunchly Catholic, and his mother wanted him to do well in school. Cristiano, however, had set his sights on the soccer world where he envisioned his future. When he was fourteen years old, Cristiano was expelled from school for getting into an argument with a teacher. When the teacher disrespected Cristiano, he threw a chair at the teacher and was immediately expelled from the school.

After that incident, his mother agreed that it would be best for Cristiano to focus entirely on soccer. Cristiano convinced his mother that he might have a chance to play soccer semi-professionally in order to earn a living. Cristiano has said that "when I got to 14, I felt I had the potential. I thought I was maybe good enough at that time to play semi-professionally." He never imagined that he would end up where he is today, as one of the top soccer players in the history of the sport.

After two successful years of playing with Nacional's youth squad, Cristiano was given a three day tryout with Sporting Lisbon, one of the best clubs in the Portuguese Professional Soccer League that regularly plays in the UEFA Champions League, which brings together the best clubs from around Europe. This was Ronaldo's chance to make his way into the high ranks of the soccer world.

But sometimes, a little bit of luck and a special friendship are also needed to break into the soccer world. Cristiano has shared that one of his closest friends, Albert Fantrau, helped him make his way into the highest ranks of European soccer. He says, "I have to thank my friend Albert for my success. We played together for a youth club. When people from Sporting (Lisbon) arrived, they told us that whoever scored more goals would be accepted to their Academy. We won that game 3-0, I scored the first goal, then Albert scored a header, and the third was a goal that impressed everyone. Albert went one on one with the goalkeeper. I was running next to him, he went round the keeper, all he needed to do was just to get the ball into the empty net. But he passed it to me and I scored. I was accepted to the Academy. After the match, I approached him and asked him "why" and he answered, "You're better than me."

After his lucky break, thanks to his friend Albert and successful three day workout, Sporting agreed to sign him to their youth academy. The Academia Sporting, the youth soccer academy of Sporting, is one of the most renowned youth soccer academy's in Europe. The majority of famous Portuguese soccer players, such as Nani, Ricardo Quaresma, Paulo Futre and Luis Figo also were fortunate enough to make their way through the

Academia Sporting before going on to successful careers in major clubs around Europe. Paulo Cardoso, his first coach at Sporting Lisbon, said: "When he got the ball he went past two or three players. At the end of the game the players gathered around him, they knew he was a special kid."

Destiny seemed to be smiling on Ronaldo. He was training in one of Europe's best youth academies and had limitless opportunities to continue to grow as a soccer player. But at the age of 15, Cristiano's soccer future was put in limbo. During a medical checkup he was diagnosed with a racing heart. This medical condition exists when the heart beats faster than normal. His racing heart threatened to make him give up his soccer career as it could have been dangerous to his health to continue playing, adding stress to an already overworking heart.

Cristiano decided to undergo an operation. A team of doctors had to use a laser to fix a part of his heart that was causing it to beat so fast. The operation was a risky one, but Cristiano wanted to take the chance.

Luckily the operation went well, and a few hours after the operation, Cristiano was released from the hospital. Only days after the operation, Cristiano was back on the field training. His determination to become one of the greatest soccer players ever gave him the motivation to rebound from a potentially life threatening medical condition.

CHAPTER THREE

THE NEW PRODIGY FOR THE LEGENDARY CLUB OF MANCHESTER UNITED

"People have to understand one thing: at the age of 18, I arrived at a dream club like Manchester United. It was a dream come true." – Cristiano Ronaldo

CAN YOU IMAGINE BEING ONLY 18 years old and suddenly being signed by one of the most historic soccer teams in all of Europe? Ronaldo, after quickly passing through the youth ranks of the Sporting Lisbon club, had captured the attention of numerous big name teams around Europe. English Premier League teams such as Arsenal and Liverpool expressed interest in Cristiano, as did the Spanish team Barcelona, ironically becoming Ronaldo´s chief rival during his years at Real Madrid almost a decade later.

Ronaldo made his professional debut for Sporting Lisbon, on October 7th, 2002. He scored two goals in this game, and his team won 2-0. In the spring of 2003, his club played against Manchester United during the inauguration of Lisbon´s new stadium. Sporting Lisbon beat Manchester United handily, and on the flight back to England, various Manchester United players urged Sir Alex Ferguson, Manchester´s legendary coach, to sign the young phenomenon.

Ferguson said that, "After we played Sporting last week, the lads in the dressing room talked about him constantly, and on the plane back from the game they urged me to sign him. That's how highly they rated him." Ferguson admitted that Ronaldo was one of the "most exciting young players" he had ever seen and only months after his professional debut in the Portuguese League, Cristiano was signed by one of Europe's most successful teams.

When he signed for Manchester United, the young Cristiano, who—only four years earlier—had been expelled from his hometown school, said "I am very happy to be signing for the best team in the world, and especially proud to be the first Portuguese player to join United."

Manchester United paid heftily for Cristiano, paying an almost 12 million Euro transfer fee which was one of the highest fees paid for such a young player in the history of the sport. But Ronaldo was unfazed by the challenge. When asked whether he was intimidated to be joining United at such a young age, he responded, "Lots of young players have triumphed at United, so why can't it happen to me? I'm not worried I'm young—it's an incentive to do the best I can."

In soccer, your uniform number says a lot about what type of player your club expects you to become. Upon arriving at Manchester United, Ronaldo was given the number 7, the same number used by other United greats such as David Beckham and George Best. Just as the young Ronaldo had benefitted by developing his game at the Sporting youth academy, he now had the chance to continue to progress as a soccer player under the support of Sir Alex Ferguson.

Sir Alex Ferguson was from Scotland, and played for several Scottish soccer teams when he was younger. He managed Manchester United from 1986 until 2013, winning 13 English Premier League titles and numerous other trophies. He is considered by many to be the greatest soccer coach of all time.

Cristiano has said that "For me, Sir Alex was my father in football. He was crucial to my career and outside football, was a great human being with me. Talent isn't everything. You can have it from the cradle, but it is necessary to learn the trade to be the best." Sir Alex helped Cristiano develop his natural talent in order to become one of the best ever.

At United, Cristiano quickly developed into the all around play maker that defines him today. His early success led some people to compare him with George Best, a former United player and legend. Best once said that "there have been a few players described as 'the new George Best' over the years, but this is the first time it's been a compliment to me."

His competitive drive to become the best player of all time, however, also led him into conflicts with other players and some of his teammates. In 2006, he received a red card for kicking Andy Cole, a former United teammate. Ruud Van Nistelrooy was a fellow striker for Manchester United who clashed frequently with Ronaldo. After frequent altercations, United decided to stick with Ronaldo and sold Van Nistelrooy to Real Madrid.

Ronaldo also clashed with Wayne Rooney, another long time teammate at United. In the 2006 World Cup, Rooney was playing for England and Ronaldo for his home country of Portugal. The two were involved in an incident which led to Rooney being sent off. Many people claimed that Ronaldo provoked Rooney and he received a lot of criticism from fans. Ronaldo asked for a transfer due to the incident, but since he was having his breakout season in that year, United didn't grant him the transfer.

Imagine that you were on track to become one of the best players in the world, but you played on a club that also had world class players that shared your position, like Van Nistelrooy and Wayne Rooney. Wouldn't it seem natural to be competitive in order to become the best player you could be? While many people have criticized Ronaldo's competitiveness, others consider it to be his most important attribute, and one that richly contributes to him being the great player that he is.

After those disputes, Ronaldo clearly became United's best player. He won his first Premier League Title during the 2006-2007 season, and then went on to score a total of 42 goals in all competitions during the 2007–08 season, helping Manchester United win the UEFA Champions League over fellow English side Chelsea.

In the 2008-2009 season, he helped Manchester United return to the Champions League final hoping to be one of the only teams to repeat as Champions League winners in back to back seasons. His team, however, lost to Barcelona, led by Lionel Messi, who would soon become the personal arch rival of Cristiano. Despite losing the Champions League Final, Cristiano won the Ballon D´or, the trophy for the world´s best soccer player. It was the first time a United Player had won the trophy since George Best won it in 1968.

If you had won numerous English Premier League trophies, a Champions League trophy, and an individual trophy for best player of the year, wouldn´t you want to try and prove your success at another club? That´s what Ronaldo decided to do following the 2008-2009 season in which he helped United win their third consecutive English Premier League title.

His coach, Sir Alex Ferguson, lamented that Cristiano would be leaving the club, but recognized that "we´ve had some great players at this club in my 20 years, but he's up with the best." Where would Ronaldo take his talent next.

CHAPTER FOUR

THE SUPERSTAR AT REAL MADRID

"It gives me the happiest feeling in the world. I just love scoring. It doesn't matter if it's a simple goal from close range, a long shot or a dribble around several players, I just love to score all types of goals." – Cristiano Ronaldo

IF YOU WERE ONE OF the world's best players, wouldn't you too be tempted to play for the world's most successful soccer team? Real Madrid, from the Spanish Professional Soccer League is arguably the most successful club in

the history of European soccer. They have accumulated a record 10 Champion's League trophies,
setting them apart as the most successful club in the history of soccer.

On June 26th, 2009, Ronaldo confirmed that he would be leaving Manchester United to begin a new challenge at Real Madrid, the club that had housed all time greats such as Alfred DiStefano, David Beckham, Zinedine Zidane, the other (Brazilian), Ronaldo, among many others.

His transfer fee was, at the time, the highest in the history of the sport at 94 million Euros. Real Madrid, not wanting to lose their prized investment, also put a one billion Euro buy-out clause on Cristiano, making sure he would stay at Madrid for years to come. During his transfer, Ronaldo said, that "I know that they (Real Madrid) are going to demand a lot of me to be successful at the club and I know that I'm going to have much more pressure than at Manchester United because I was there for many years, but it means a new challenge and it is going to help me be the best footballer."

Cristiano's arrival to the Spanish Professional League was also the beginning of his great rivalry with Lionel Messi, the Argentinean soccer player who was developing as a star with Barcelona, Real Madrid's chief contender in the Spanish League. After Cristiano's first season at Madrid, he finished second in voting for the FIFA Ballon D'or behind Lionel Messi. Messi would go on to win the award for four straight years, with Cristiano finishing runner-up behind Messi before eventually winning the award himself two years in a row, in 2014 and 2015.

His second season at Madrid proved to be

his breakout year as he set the goal scoring record for a single season. The crowds at the Santiago Bernabeu, Madrid's famous stadium, were sure that they had found a star that would bring them back to greatness. He ended the season by scoring two goals in the final match, taking his scoring total to 40 goals in a single La Liga season. He was the only person at the time to have scored over 40 goals in a single season.

During that record breaking year, Ronaldo scored at a rate equaling one goal scored every 70 minutes that he was on the field. Imagine that! Most of us would be happy if we were to score a goal every once in awhile, but Ronaldo was averaging more than a goal per game!

During the 2011-2012 season, Ronaldo's third season at Madrid, he helped his team win the Spanish League trophy. Barcelona had won the trophy the previous seasons, and taking back the trophy from their arch enemies was an accomplishment very important to the Madrid fans.

Madrid ended the season with a record 100 points, proving that their squad was one of the best teams in the history of the Spanish League. On a personal level, Cristiano broke his own record by scoring 46 goals in the Spanish League and a total of 60 goals in all competitions. It seemed like the only one he was competing against for his goal scoring records was himself!

At the beginning of the 2013-2014 season, Ronaldo began to express certain frustrations. After scoring two goals during the first game of the season, he didn't celebrate them as he usually did. He said after the game that he was unhappy for "professional reasons." Some speculated that he was unhappy because he lost the Ballon D'or award to Lionel Messi for the third straight season.

His coach at the time, José Mourinho, said that, "if Messi is the best on the planet, Ronaldo is the best in the universe. If you are going to give out the Ballon d'Or because a player is the best, give it to Cristiano or Messi. But I ask, if the two are on the same level, is it normal that one wins four and the other one? It is not." The controversy surrounding the rivalry between Messi and Ronaldo was gaining a lot of media attention. At the end of that season, Ronaldo once again finished second in voting for the FIFA Ballon D´or behind Messi.

FIFA´s president at the time, Sepp Blatter, added fuel to the fire regarding the rivalry between Messi and Ronaldo during a news conference during the season. Blatter praised Messi´s quiet and humble demeanor and style of play, while criticizing Ronaldo for being a "commander" on the field. He also poked fun of Ronaldo´s hairstyles, saying that "one of them has more expenses for the hairdresser than the other." Ronaldo, however, played the rivalry by saying this of his comparisons to Messi, "Messi and me?? It's like a Ferrari and a Porsche!"

After not winning any trophies during the 2013-2014 season, many people in the media thought that Ronaldo might be leaving Real Madrid. He said at the time that, "I´m proud to play for Real Madrid because I have fun; when you no longer have fun it's a sign that it's time to leave. For now though, I'm happy here at the greatest club in the world."

However, his team signed another great striker that off season named Gareth Bale. Bale´s transfer fee was reportedly higher than the price the team paid for Cristiano a few years earlier. After months of speculation,

Cristiano decided to stay at Madrid and signed a contract that made him the highest paid player in the sport. He was to receive more than 17 million Euros a season!

Cristiano's decision to stay at Madrid paid off mightily, because though they finished third in the Spanish League season, they won the Champion's League by beating their cross-town rivals of Athletic Madrid. "La Décima" means "tenth" in Spanish, and Madrid's fans had long dreamt of winning their tenth Champion's League trophy. In the final against Athletic, Ronaldo scored the goal to clinch their win. He finished the tournament with a record 17 goals in the Champion's League. He also became the first player in the history of the league to have scored a goal in a Champion's League final while playing in different European leagues.

Ronaldo almost missed the most important

game of his career at Madrid due to an injury that had sidelined him for various games near the end of the season. Ronaldo explained that, "In your life you do not win without sacrifices and you must take risks. If I had stopped I would have been fine. I did not want to miss the final of the Champion's League. I was not fully fit, but I forced the issue." His determination to help his team helped him overcome his injury problems.

Earlier in that same season Ronaldo had said that, "I never promise anything. I don't promise anything to my mum. I don't promise anything to the supporters." Despite saying that, the fans at the Santiago Bernabeu stadium were ecstatic that Ronaldo helped bring Madrid their tenth Champion's League trophy.

That year, Ronaldo also won the FIFA Ballon D'or, taking the award away from

Lionel Messi who finished second this time around. Ronaldo would go on to win the award again the following year, making him one of the only players in the world to have won the award for the best player in the world three times.

On October 17th, 2015, Ronaldo became Real Madrid's all-time leading goal scorer by passing Real Madrid legend Raúl. He currently is the third all-time scorer in the history of the Spanish League as he continues to score goals at record-breaking pace. His current coach, the former Madrid player Zinedine Zidane, has said that, "When you play with Ronaldo on your team you are already 1-0 up," attesting to the greatness of Cristiano.

Despite outstanding success at Real Madrid, many people consider that Real Madrid and Ronaldo are still second behind Barcelona and Messi. During Cristiano's time at Real Madrid, he has only helped Real win one Spanish League title, while Barcelona has won five. One thing is for sure, though: the rivalry between Barcelona and Real Madrid (and Cristiano and Messi) has been a major storyline in the sport's world that we hope will continue to intrigue us for years to come.

CHAPTER FIVE

THE HOPE OF HIS HOME COUNTRY OF PORTUGAL

"To me, being the best means proving it in different countries and championships." – Cristiano Ronaldo

EVERY SOCCER PLAYER DREAMS OF one day winning the World Cup Trophy for his or her country. Ronaldo had already won the Champion's League with a team from England and a team from Spain. He had won the

English Premier League, the Spanish Professional League and a number of other smaller trophies with his clubs. On an individual level, he had been crowned best player in the league three times. The one major accomplishment that he was missing in his career was winning a trophy for his country.

But soccer is a team game, and one player can only do so much. Cristano's home country of Portugal is a small country, and while it has produced some high quality players over the years, it isn't on the same level of countries such as Brazil, Argentina, Germany, or Italy; countries that are much bigger and produce many more quality players. If Cristiano were able to win a major trophy for his country, it would be an incredible accomplishment.

Cristiano was first given a chance to represent his country on the Portuguese National team as part of the under-15 team while he was still playing for Sporting Lisbon. After moving to England and proving himself at Manchester United, Ronaldo moved up through the ranks representing also the under-17, under-20, under-21, and the under-23 national sides. He scored at least one goal for each of these teams.

On August 20th, 2003, Ronaldo made his first appearance for the Portuguese senior national team in a 1–0 victory against Kazakhstan. The next year, Portugal made a great showing at the 2004 European Championships. Ronaldo scored his first goal for Portugal during that tournament as well as scoring the decisive goal in the semifinal win against the Netherlands. Portugal eventually lost to Greece in the final, but the fact that they made it to the final over traditional powerhouses such as England, Italy and Germany brought a lot of pride to Ronaldo's home country.

The next major competition was the 2006 World Cup. During the qualification stages, Ronaldo was the second-highest scorer in the European zone with seven goals, helping make sure his country secured a spot in the world's most important soccer competition.

Portugal performed well during the tournament and advanced easily past their group stage. In their quarter final match against England, however, Ronaldo was involved in a situation that involved Wayne Rooney, his club teammate at Manchester United. When Rooney was whistled for a foul for stepping on a Portuguese defender, Cristiano complained aggressively to the referee who eventually showed Rooney a red card. After Rooney was sent off, Cristiano was seen winking to Portugal's bench and many speculated that he had unfairly influenced the referee to get his club teammate sent off.

Portugal won the game against England, but lost in the semifinals to France as Cristiano was heavily booed by the crowd.

In 2008, leading up to the next World Cup, the Portuguese coach Carlos Queiroz recognized the talent and leadership in Ronaldo and named him the new permanent captain of the Portugal national team.

During the 2010 World Cup, Ronaldo was determined to redeem himself and bring his country the long awaited World Cup trophy. During group play, he was named man of the match in all three group matches against Côte d'Ivoire   (0–0), North   Korea (7–0) and Brazil (0–0). The tie against Brazil, who was a favorite to win the World Cup that year, brought confidence to the Portuguese national team.

Their luck ran out, however, when they

were seeded to face Spain in the round of 16. Ronaldo played well but missed several chances for a goal. The Spanish national team was in great form, and knocked Portugal out before eventually winning the World Cup. After losing to Spain, Ronaldo stated that, "I will only be fully content with my career when I have lifted a trophy with Portugal."

During the 2012 European Cup, Ronaldo again carried his team through the group stages and into the semi-final against the same Spanish squad that had knocked them out of the last World Cup. This time, which was the semi-final, the game ended in a draw and went to penalty kicks. Strangely enough, Ronaldo was set to kick last, but since his other teammate's didn´t net their penalty kicks and the Spanish side did, Ronaldo didn´t even get to take a penalty kick. Once again, Spain had dashed its neighbor's dreams of winning a major international competition.

In 2014, Ronaldo scored two goals in Portugal's 5–1 win over Cameroon during a friendly match. Those two goals took his goal total to 49 goals, thus making him his country's all-time leading goal scorer.

Ronaldo was getting older, however, and his chances to win a major trophy for his country were running out. He knew that one of his last chances to succeed for his country was at the 2014 World Cup in Brazil.

Unfortunately, Ronaldo wasn't in top shape when the World Cup started. He was suffering from tendonitis and muscular injuries to his thighs after suffering through the end of the Spanish Professional League during the 2013-2014 season.

When asked why he decided to play at the World Cup despite clearly being injured, Ronaldo stated; "If we had two or three

Cristiano Ronaldo's on the team I would feel more comfortable. But we don't." His competitive desire to help his country win even made him put his own club career in jeopardy by playing with an injury.

Portugal had bad luck in the group stage as they were drawn to play in a group led by Germany (the eventual champions), the United States and the powerful African squad of Ghana. Despite tying the United States and beating Ghana with the help of a goal from Cristiano, Portugal didn't advance out of the group. Ronaldo became the first Portuguese player to score in three World Cup tournaments, but his dream of winning a major championship is still on hold.

CHAPTER SIX

THE SOCCER PLAYER IN HIS OWN CATEGORY

"There is no harm in dreaming of becoming the world's best player. It is all about trying to be the best. I will keep working hard to achieve it, but it is within my capabilities." – Cristiano Ronaldo

VERY SELDOM DO WE COME across a player who combines natural athleticism, otherworldly tactical skill, and an unbending desire to continually improve. Can you imagine standing at 6 feet 2 inches tall and not having an ounce of body fat? Cristiano has been described as having one of the most athletic bodies in the sport, but his distinction as one of the greatest players of history comes from his determination to always push himself to get better.

Ryan Giggs was a long time player at Manchester United who played into his 40´s. He played alongside Cristiano for a few years and said that, "When he (Cristiano) gets the ball, you can just leave him to it while he beats player after player." Almost all of his former coaches have also recognized Ronaldo´s ability to take over games, and have devised technical schemes to take the most advantage of his ability. Eusebio, another famous soccer player has said that, "He has magic in his boots. The first thing you notice about him is that he is incredibly quick and very, very powerful for such a young man. He has great, close control and his technique is excellent. He believes he can do anything with the ball, and that confidence makes him very special indeed."

Cristiano has always played an attacking role, either as a center striker or as a winger. Though his preferred position is on the left wing, he has developed himself as a versatile attacker capable of playing in any offensive position. When playing alongside other quality strikers such as Karim Benzema and Gareth Bale—like he currently does at Real Madrid—it is important to be able to adapt your game to be able to play alongside such quality talent.

Cristiano is known for his ability when he has the ball at his feet. He has extremely quick and dynamic pace, is a fantastic dribbler, and is one of the best finishers in the game with an extremely powerful kick. However, he is also known for having good vision and positioning.

He seems to have an otherworldly ability to predict plays and be in the right spot at the right time. His soccer intelligence helps him to be in position to score goals.

Cristiano´s two most recognized attributes are his ability to beat players in a one on one situation, and his ability to score goals from free kick situations. Many people are left in awe as he passes defender after defender. His powerful, bending shots from free kick situations are also well known. Many goal keepers tremble when they´re facing a Ronaldo free kick. His free kick speed is about 130 kilometers per hour, which is compared roughly with the speed of a space shuttle while launching. Imagine being a goalie trying to stop a space shuttle coming at you!

Since he is so tall and athletic, many of his goals also come from his height. He is able to rise above defenders to score many goals from corner kicks and other set pieces. He is said to have a jumping ability that surpasses that of the average NBA player.

In 2014, Ronaldo was named one of the fastest football players in the world. Usain Bolt, the Jamaican sprinter who has won gold in three consecutive Olympic Games, and who holds the world record for the 100 meter and 200 meter sprints, once said, "I fear no one on the track. Maybe if Ferrari Ronaldo comes on the track I may tremble."

When Ronaldo arrived at Manchester United as a teenager, he was skinny and weak. He decided to focus on improving his strength and over the following years underwent a major body transformation, into a muscular and strong player. His strength is one of the attributes that allow him to ward off defenders and keep possession of the ball. Ronaldo lifts around 23,055 kilograms of weight during a training session, which is a total of 16 Toyota Prius cars. His current coach, Zinedine Zidane, has praised Ronaldo's work ethic and continuous dedication to improving his game at practice and at the gym. Arnold Schwarzenegger, a world class body builder, has said he thinks Ronaldo is one of the fittest athletes in the world.

Alex Ferguson, his old coach at Manchester, reflected recently on Ronaldo's growth as a player. He said, "Maturity brings many things. I see some of his decision-making in terms of passing was brilliant. One-touch passing, good crosses. In the six years we had him, you just saw his game grow all the time, and he was a fantastic player. Now you see the complete player. His decision-making, his maturity, his experience, plus all the great skills he has got, they all make him the complete player."

Despite being recognized as one of soccer's greatest players of all time, Cristiano Ronaldo has also faced some tough criticism from the media. During his years at Manchester, his coach and teammates sometimes lamented that he played selfishly and was overly flamboyant. They said that he preferred to pass a defender dribbling by himself, rather than making a pass to a teammate. But as Ronaldo matured, he also improved his passing game, and during the 2006-2007 season, he had a total of 19 assists.

Ronaldo has also been criticized for having a certain arrogance while on the field. Ronaldo has been quoted as saying "I know that if I score we're going to win the match." In 2016, he received a lot of criticism when he said that the reason his team was losing was because his teammates, "...were not up to his standard."

Also in 2016, he told a Spanish newspaper that, "...there are people out there who hate me and who say I'm arrogant, vain and whatever. That's all part of my success. I am made to be the best." He continued, by saying "We cannot live being obsessed with what other people think about us. It's impossible to live like that. Not even God managed to please the entire world."

While some people see arrogance in a statement like that, Ronaldo has tried to explain that this is not arrogance, but rather part of his competitive nature. He wants to win always, and this desire many times leads him to push his teammates to be the best they can be. Real Madrid president Florentino Pérez has said, "If you are the best player in the world, you may be excused for being arrrogant."

Furthermore, Ronaldo is also oftentimes criticized for diving while trying to draw fouls. His ex-coach, José Mourinho, however, believes that, "Ronaldo is not protected by anybody, or because of anybody. Rivals see the body of an animal and they kick him. To get a yellow card they need to do that a lot." Because of his athletic build and his competitive nature, he is often targeted by defenders and receives lots of hard fouls.

Cristiano is undoubtedly one of the greatest players of all time and his greatness has caused some people to criticize his game and his character. He has even recognized that, "I have my flaws too, but I am a professional who doesn't like to miss or lose." Despite all the criticism that he takes from the media and others around the soccer world, Cristiano says, "I know I'm a good professional and I know that no one's harder on me than myself and that's never going to change, under any circumstances.

CHAPTER SEVEN

THE HUMAN BEING OFF OF THE FIELD

*"Without football (soccer), my life is worth nothing." –
Cristiano Ronaldo*

IT IS EASY TO FORGET that Cristiano
Ronaldo has a life off of the soccer field. As we
watch him as week in and week out he lights
up the highlight reels with amazing goals, we
tend to forget that he is also a father, a son and
a person involved in numerous charitable
activities around the world.

Cristiano's father was one of the first people to get him involved with the game of soccer. He took on a job as an equipment manager of a local club to help his young son be able to play organized soccer. Cristiano's father, however, struggled with alcohol, and in 2005, he died from alcoholism which had caused a severe liver disease. He was only 52 years old at the time. After his father's death, Cristiano said, "Whenever I win awards, I think of my father."

Because of his father's battles with alcohol, Ronaldo has made the decision to not drink alcohol himself. In 2008, a British tabloid accused him of drinking heavily at a nightclub. Cristiano sued the newspaper for false reporting and received a financial settlement when the newspaper recognized that the story wasn't true.

Ronaldo has also had run-ins with the law.

Only a month after his father died, he was arrested for supposedly raping a woman in a hotel in London. Cristiano maintained his innocence and charges were eventually dropped due to insufficient evidence. After being released, he said, "I have always strongly maintained my innocence of any wrong-doing, and I am glad that this matter is at an end so that I can concentrate on playing for Manchester United."

We often hear about famous athletes who have children with many different women leaving those children to be raised by single mothers. Ronaldo, on the contrary, is a single father. He became a father on June 17th, 2010, to a boy he named Cristiano. Little Cristiano was born in the United States, and Ronaldo, despite never revealing the identity of the mother, has full custody of his son and calls him Cristianinho. He has said, "I think it's the best thing in life to have a kid." He also hopes that his son can follow in his footsteps as a world class soccer player. "I want my son to be a player. I am a footballer and I want him to be one too," he has said.

Ronaldo has dated famous models throughout his lifetime. For five years, from 2010 to 2015, he dated a Russian model named Irina Shayk. Both Ronaldo and Shayk did commercials for the famous brand of clothing called Armani Exchange. For almost five years, the couple was followed by the press. In 2014, they appeared together on the cover of Vogue magazine. However, in early 2015, they ended their relationship.

Cristiano is a Roman Catholic and many of his charitable activities are a result of his faith. He donates blood many times during the year to help others, and for that reason he doesn't have any tattoos which would prevent him from being able to donate blood.

While many athletes decide to share their wealth with others, Cristiano is a philanthropist who has devoted his wealth and his fame to help numerous causes around the world. After a tsunami killed close to 250,000 people in Indonesia in 2004, Ronaldo visited the area to help raise funds for reconstruction. His desire to help the people of Indonesia came after television footage showed a stranded eight year old boy wearing a Cristiano Ronaldo jersey after being hit by the tsunami. Even after almost a decade, Cristiano still maintains his connection to Indonesia. He currently is ambassador for The Mangrove Care Forum in Indonesia, an organization aiming to help preserve mangrove forests.

Cristiano´s mother is a cancer survivor, and after she was released from the hospital, Cristiano donated close to 150,000 Euros to the hospital that saved her life so that they could build a cancer center on his home island in Portugal. In 2012, Ronaldo paid for specialist treatment for a nine-year-old boy from the Canary Island who apparently had terminal cancer.

Despite being an international star with homes in Spain, New York City and other places, Cristiano still maintains a close relationship with his hometown of Madeira. In 2010, a major flood affected the people of Madeira. After the flood, Cristiano appeared in a charity soccer match to raise funds to help people affected by the flood.

Cristiano has even sold some of his most valuable trophies won as a soccer player for humanitarian causes. In 2011, he won the golden boot as Europe's top goal scorer for the season. A year later he sold the boot for 1.5 million Euros and donated all of that money to help build schools for Palestinian children in

Gaza, an area in perpetual warfare.

Cristiano also participates in other humanitarian causes. He participates in programs to help children and teenagers around the world avoid drug addiction, HIV, malaria and obesity. In 2013, he began working with Save the Children helping the fight against child hunger and obesity. Recently, Ronaldo has helped the fight against Ebola, a deadly disease that affects thousands of people, mostly in Africa.

If you were one of the world's best soccer players, would you devote as much time and energy to humanitarian causes as Ronaldo does? Cristiano has stated that he would rather be remembered as a role model than one of world football's best players.

He understands, staying, "We should make the most of life, enjoy it because that's the way it is!" Soccer is important, but it is only one part of his life. He has said that he believes in living a relaxed lifestyle and likes to, "...spend my free time with family and friends, which keeps me relaxed and in a positive mind-set." A player who—despite being an international phenomenon—still devotes so much time, energy and money to help people around the world, should hardly be considered arrogant.

CHAPTER EIGHT

THE CELEBRITY OF POPULAR CULTURE

"People are envious of me because I'm rich, handsome and a great player." – Cristiano Ronaldo

OUR SOCIETY IS FASCINATED BY wealth and fame, and Cristiano has both. He is perhaps the most popular face in the sports world and his celebrity reputation extends to all different parts of our popular culture.

Like other famous athletes, the majority of Cristiano´s wealth comes from endorsements and advertising campaigns, rather than from his salary for playing soccer. During the 2014-2015 season, Ronaldo reportedly earned over 79 million dollars from his salary and from other off-field earnings. This made him the second richest athlete in the world, behind only the famous boxer Floyd Mayweather Junior. The finance magazine Forbes, regularly rates Ronaldo as one of the world´s wealthiest athletes.

Because of his fame on the soccer field, many big companies seek him out as the face of their products. Ronaldo is considered to be one of the world's most marketable athletes. In 2014, he was considered to be the most recognized athlete in the world and also named by Time Magazine as one of the 100 most influential people in the world. This recognition has helped him gain numerous advertising jobs for different companies.

He currently has sponsorship deals with Nike, the famous athletic sportswear company, and wears Nike soccer boots for all of his games. Beginning in 2010, Nike created a boot just for Cristiano, called the CR7 line. Just like in the basketball world, having your own sports shoe is considered the ultimate prestige. The Mercurial Superfly CR7 boots are one of the best selling soccer shoes on the market.

But Cristiano´s image sells much more than just soccer shoes. He also has endorsement deals with such companies as Coca Cola and Emporio Armani. His image of style and wealth have landed him deals with the watch maker Tag Heuer, different international banks, cell phone companies, restaurants, airlines and online gambling sites like Pokerstars. He has also been featured on the cover of numerous soccer related video games.

He is considered to be one of the best looking athletes around the world, and he knows that his image is coveted by other men and admired by women around the world. His former teammate Wayne Rooney once said, "In the time I've been playing with Ronnie, the one thing I've noticed about him is that he can't walk past his reflection without admiring it, even if we're about to play a game of football."

Because of that famous image, Cristiano is also a fashion icon and is sought after by numerous prestigious clothing designers, fashion magazines, fitness and exercise companies, hair stylists, and perfume and cosmetic specialists. He promotes numerous fashion companies, including the famed Armani Exchange.

In 2006, Cristiano even opened up his own fashion store. He called it CR7, and it first opened on his home island of Madeira in Portugal. From there, his business expanded into Lisbon, the capital of Portugal. His fashion boutique sells expensive high fashion clothes items, including, diamond-studded belts, jeans with leather pockets, and patented buckled loafers. He has also designed his own range of underwear and socks, premium shirts and shoes, and his own fragrance, in partnership with Eden Parfums.

On the internet, Ronaldo is also widely followed. Some of you may even follow him on Facebook or subscribe to his Twitter account. He is considered the most popular online athlete in the world, beating out other famous athletes like Kobe Bryant, Lionel Messi and Lebron James. While the average person on Facebook has only 200 friends, Cristiano has well over 100 million people following him on Facebook, and close to 40 million on Twitter! Including Twitter and

Instagram, he has close to 160 million following him on the online world. Only the singer Shakira reached 100 million followers faster than Cristiano.

Since he has so much fame and popularity on the internet, Ronaldo has released different apps for smart phones. In 2011, he released a game for iPhones called, "Heads up with Cristiano." The game is obviously related to soccer. Two years later in 2013, he created a social networking site called Viva Ronaldo.

Because so many people want to know the details of Cristiano's life, many people have written about him. His own autobiography is called "Moments," and was published in 2007 when he was still playing for Manchester United. A made-for-TV movie called, "Tested to the Limit." was produced in 2011. In the movie, Ronaldo is tested both physically and mentally, to show his stamina and strength.

Other documentaries have also been produced about Cristiano's life and his achievements, most notably "Cristiano Ronaldo: The World at his Feet," in 2014, and another simply called "Ronaldo," in 2015.

Even though he is still actively playing, Ronaldo has his own museum! The Museum called Museu CR7, opened in 2013 in his hometown of Funchal, Madeira. It contains exhibits that include his numerous trophies, as well as memorabilia of his playing career. If he continues to win trophies at the current pace, he may need to expand the museum!

On a national level, Cristiano has been recognized by the president of Portugal, Anibal Cavaco, as a Grand Officer of the Order of Prince Henry. This distinction is given to famous Portuguese people who have achieved great fame around the world. President Cavaco said that the award was given to Cristiano, "To distinguish an athlete of world renown who has been a symbol of Portugal globally, contributing to the international projection of the country and setting an example of tenacity for future generations."

Ronaldo is also only one of four soccer players—along with Steven Gerrard, Pelé and David Beckham—who have a statue of wax made after his likeness at the famous Madame Tussauds Wax Museum in London. It would seem that Cristiano's fame extends even beyond our galaxy, because in 2015, astronomers from an observatory in Portugal discovered a previously unknown galaxy. They named it Cosmos Redshift 7, but shortened it to CR7 as a tribute to Cristiano Ronaldo's initials and uniform number. Can you imagine having a galaxy named after you? Cristiano is definitely out of this world!

Living a life of fame comes with its own challenges. Cristiano has recognized that as well, saying, "I have practically no private life. I'm already used to this and ready for it. Yes, sometimes it is hard, but it is the choice I made." His success on the soccer field, coupled with his widely recognized image and demeanor, has turned him into a cultural celebrity recognized around the world.

Alan Barry, a European sports commentator, once remarked about Cristiano, that he is "...a gift from heaven, he is truly a gift from heaven. Whatever he touches turns to gold." Numerous companies have found that to be true, as his image helps sell billions of dollars of merchandise.

CHAPTER NINE

ONE OF THE ALL TIME GREATS OF THE SOCCER WORLD

"There is no point in making predictions. It´s not worth speculating about because nothing is set in stone and things change all the time in football (soccer). – Cristiano Ronaldo

THERE WILL LIKELY NEVER AGAIN be a player who has brought together Ronaldo´s unique combination of physical strength, outstanding athletic ability, world renowned image and competitive desire to be the best he can be. When he eventually does decide to hang up his soccer boots and retire, people will remember him as the all-time leading scorer at one of the world's most prestigious clubs, Real Madrid. They will remember him for the two Champion's League titles that he helped his teams win (and maybe more to come), his numerous individual awards, and also for his celebrity status.

Luis Figo, a former Portuguese soccer star has said that "there are some things Ronaldo can do with a football that make me touch my head and wonder how on earth he did it. Many of us can share in that feeling. After more than a decade of success, Cristiano has said, "I don't have to show anything to anyone. There is nothing left to prove." He understands that there have been few soccer players in the history of the game that have achieved what he has achieved. Yet, at the same time, he remarks, "I'm aware that, whatever the circumstances, there will always be speculation about me." Despite being one of the greatest players in the history of the game, he also suffers lots of criticism, but perhaps that comes with being a world class soccer player.

Other people believe that Cristiano's legacy has been overshadowed because he has played at the same time (and in the same league) as Lionel Messi, who is widely considered to be the best ever. The rivalry between Messi and Ronaldo is compared to other great sports rivalries such as Muhammad Ali versus Joe Frazier in the boxing world, or Michael Jordan versus Magic Johnson in the basketball world. Even Ronaldinho—Messi's former teammate—has joined in the debate by saying, "Cristiano Ronaldo is the most complete player I have ever seen, and my son adores him."

Can the soccer world accept two great soccer stars at the same time? Cristiano has said of the comparison with Messi, "...part of my life now. People are bound to compare us. He tries to do his best for his club and for his national team, as I do, and there is a degree of rivalry with both of us trying to do the best for the teams we represent."

Messi and Ronaldo are fantastic soccer players, having shared the FIFA Ballon D´or between them for the last 7 years, and 8 of the last 9 years. For almost a decade, the world´s best soccer player has either been Cristiano or Messi. The "Clasico" is one of the most widely watched sporting events in the world, when Messi´s Barcelona teams plays against Cristiano´s Real Madrid squad. Despite being constantly compared to Messi, Cristiano says, "We have to look on this rivalry with a positive spirit, because it's a good thing."

Cristiano Ronaldo has very little left to prove in the world of soccer. He has given the soccer world years of amazing highlights and record setting performances. He has transformed the game and brought it new popularity to different audiences around the world.

But his influence has gone beyond just the soccer field. He is one of the most recognizable faces of our popular culture, and is seen everywhere from perfume commercials to underwear ads. He has used his fame to sponsor numerous humanitarian causes, and has shared his enormous wealth with others less fortunate around the world.

When Cristiano eventually does decide to retire (and we hope that won't happen anytime soon), he will undoubtedly be remembered as one of the greatest soccer players ever, but also as a quality human being who made our world a better place.

Made in the USA
San Bernardino, CA
05 April 2017